AF488338

PERSPECTIVES FROM POISONS

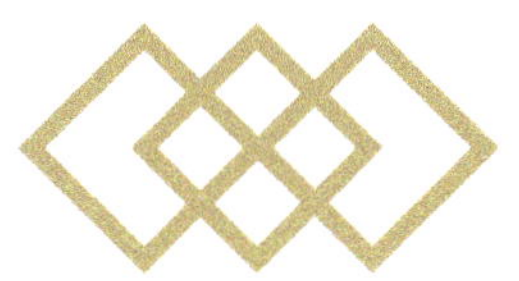

PERSPECTIVES FROM POISONS

By

Samantha Mineroff

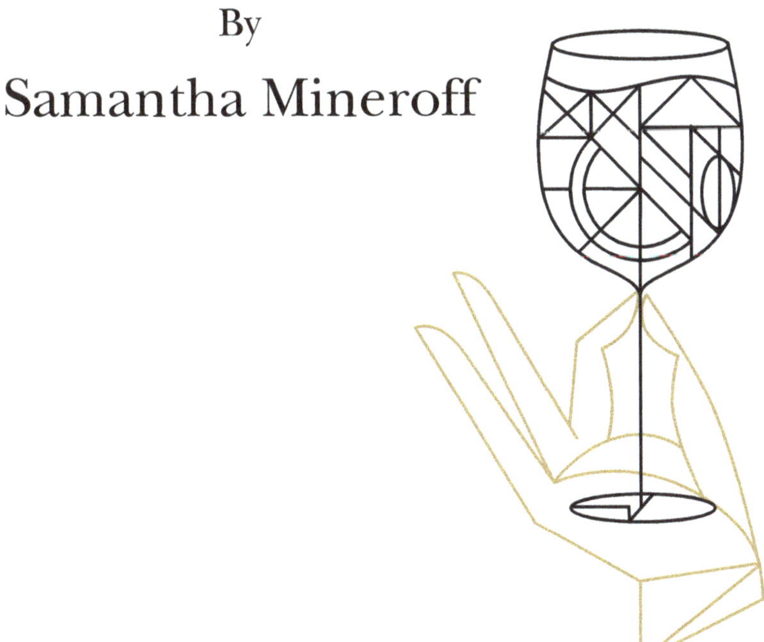

ISBN: 979-8-9907612-4-7 (hardcover)
ISBN: 979-8-9907612-2-3 (paperback)

PICK YOUR POISON

Foreword vii
Welcome to the Speakeasy xi

WINE 1
    Pinot Noir 3
    Cabernet 5
    Prosecco 7
    Sake 9
    Merlot 11
    Pinot Grigio 13
    Rosé 15
    Sauvignon Blanc 17
    Chardonnay 19
    Riesling 21

SPIRITS 23
    Elderflower Liqueur 25
    Gin 27
    Vodka Tonic 29
    Aperol 31
    Limoncello 33
    Espresso Martini 35
    Cosmopolitan 37
    Rye 39
    Scotch on the Rocks 41

Bourbon 43

Rum & Coke 45

Fireball 47

Tequila 49

Absinthe 51

BEER 53

Guinness 55

IPA 57

Pumpkin Ale 59

Kölsch 61

Stella Artois 63

Belgium Blonde Ale 65

Porter 67

Sour 69

THE HANGOVER 71

The Next Mourning 73

Sun Drunk 75

Whiskey Dreams 77

Simple Syrup 79

Sober Sex 81

Cold Showers 83

Hungover in Bed with You 85

Touch Me when I'm Low 87

Greasy Food 89

The Walk Home from the Bar 91

Secrets from the Speakeasy 95

Acknowledgements 97

About the Author 99

FOREWORD

It's a relatively well-known cliché that writers and creatives have vices to which they fall victim, particularly alcohol. We might refer to the famous aphorism, "Write drunk, edit sober," though whether or not that is sound advice I cannot say. What I can say is that alcohol, like many other complex things in life, can be taken to extremes. It can make for sweet memories or embarrassing, nightmarish moments. It can be an art that takes years of patience, focus, and attention to form, or it can drown you with swift shots. It can embellish a moment or a feeling, or it can ruin your life. Either way, it's an artistically crafted poison (with a paradoxical history of being more hygienic than water), and many of us enjoy it.

Wine has made me feel attractive, seductive, and smart. It has been the go-to drink I would imbibe in when I would try to impress my crush. Vodka was, at times, a blanket of warmth before trenching through a winter storm to get to a party where I'd try to break out of my shell. Whiskey made me daring; beer, casual. Of course, there were times where the drink went too far, and I found myself in dark echoes of the past, wondering, wondering, wondering.

Then I toured distilleries and wineries. I learned that there is much more to alcohol than just drinking it. Every type of drink has a story; each are developed in ways that naturally parallel art. They are perfected with time and aging, and different environments bring out unique flavors. Many of us drink a glass of merlot without realizing the hands, minds, earth, and barrels that went into it. We may cringe at the taste of an exceptionally strong bourbon without waiting for a hint of smokiness to come through and take us someplace new.

As humans, we are so quick to grab what's gratifying. We drink because it feels good, or at least makes us feel less bad. We drink to celebrate or to comfort ourselves in heartbreak. Some of us drink to excess, some not at all. It can make or break relationships; it can be seen as a delicacy or the devil.

And while all these poems have an underlying theme of alcohol, poison can be taken in various forms—toxic relationships, infatuation that makes you wear the rose-colored glasses, bad habits, overindulgence, and more.

It's impossible to fully understand our vices in all their forms, but rather than trying to define them, I decided to give them life. These poems are the thoughts our drinks have as we sip (or drown in) them. What if they could see us from the outside? After all, we turn to them during our vulnerable moments. They have seen us at our lowest, at our highest, at when we're our most peaceful or sad.

Some of these poems were written from personal experience, some fictional. I drew from my own exploration with alcohol, the ways it made me feel worse or better, the times where I took a break from it, the times where I fell victim to other types of vices, the memories that they brought during celebratory moments. Some of these poems may have been written under the influence, some not. Regardless, editing these with a sober and curious eye has made me appreciate the way a craft like a cocktail or wine takes time, precision, and curiosity.

Let's become more in tune with how we appreciate what's at our fingertips: the meals, the root vegetables, the soap in our hands as we wash up or wind down.

The world is full of color and personality, and not always in positive ways. But rather than run away from it, let's embrace it and explore. What can we learn about these vices? How can we defy them and not just rely on them? How can we view them from a distance? How can we look closer?

Whatever your drink of choice is, sit back, relax, and enjoy. We're in for a ride.

WELCOME TO THE SPEAKEASY

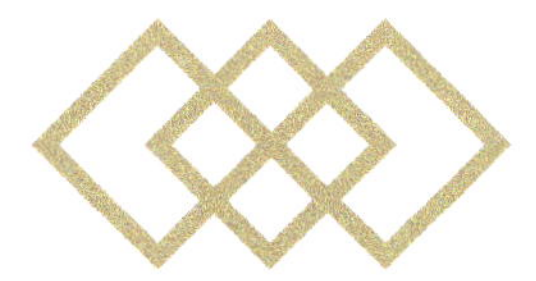

WINE

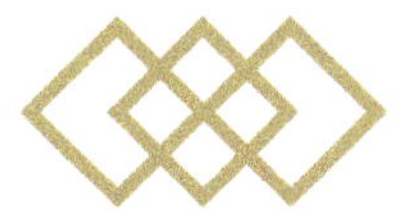

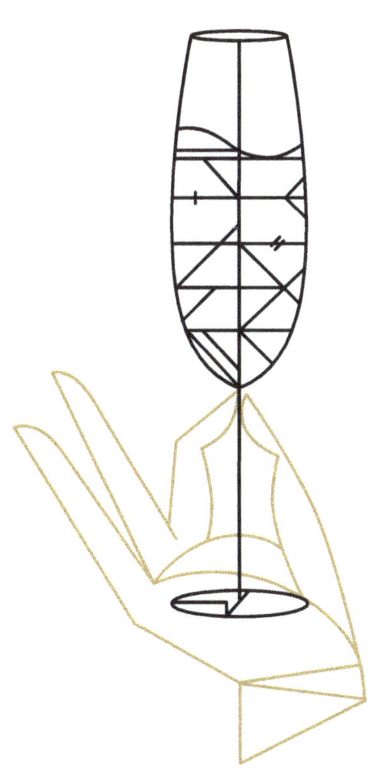

PINOT NOIR

Fingers grasp at my slender neck
she pulls me up—big, red petal lips.
Studies me on the inside as if I'm lying to her.
She pours my blood. It sits heavy in a wide
cup.
She sits. Stares.
Rubs her mouth against the rim.
Runs a hand down her leg—curvy body, like mine.
    And she wonders if the people
around her—
    glowing, warm, laughing—
know what it's like to blush
    as if to bleed from the inside.

CABERNET

Slow down—you're doing it wrong,
You move too fast—all women know that.

You used to overlook me with vague disinterest
Until the day—or was it night?—came when there was nothing
    left to drink.

And then you made the mistake—as usual—of underestimating
    me. It came back to
Bite you with ripe
Bittersweetness—
You'll come to learn that the quality of us should be enjoyed
    slowly.
We won't disappoint.

PROSECCO

By day,
    I'm a cool breeze; you
Barely see me coming until you
    Softly sleep on the train ride home.
By night, I'm the electricity you were seeking all week, making
    Her knees weak
While *you* try and play it cool.

Lick your lips, linger. Warm her cheeks
And wonder if you've had one too many
Or not enough.

    Is it lust or is it me? Will the jealousy
Ever be too much—
Or will you keep asking for more than you should?

SAKE

In a brilliant and confusing way
    You reflected—not quite as beautiful as a diamond—
the things that held me back, instead of had my back. You showed
    me more than a few ways a person can be
taken advantage of.
My anger has been dispersed across all the ways I had been
stripped of my youth. Old souls are formed—
but I always took it as a compliment.

Gentle, caring, I understood to the point that it became
    nonsensical.

But, as I was raised to be, I remained smart,
and now, it's like
I became an expert in the wrong textbook that we all followed
    for safety.

A manual instead of a novel to manifest dreams,
    stretching my timeline until I could come clean.
Spill a bloody truth like a poured drink.

WINEMAKING PROCESS

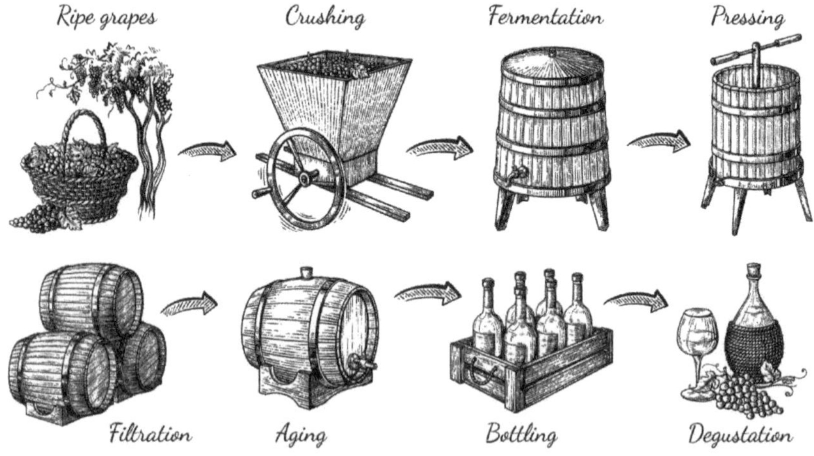

MERLOT

In the many moments where I waited and watched, longing for
     someone to see my beauty,
I realized I had a truth-telling serum that no one wanted to touch.

And it hurts,
     stories tucked inside.

Somewhere in this band's beginning chords, I remember you—
     a proper dinner and a show
—signing off with my first affogato.

I should've known
this would be just bitter and sweet. I melted, ice cream,
under a powerful force
I didn't understand.

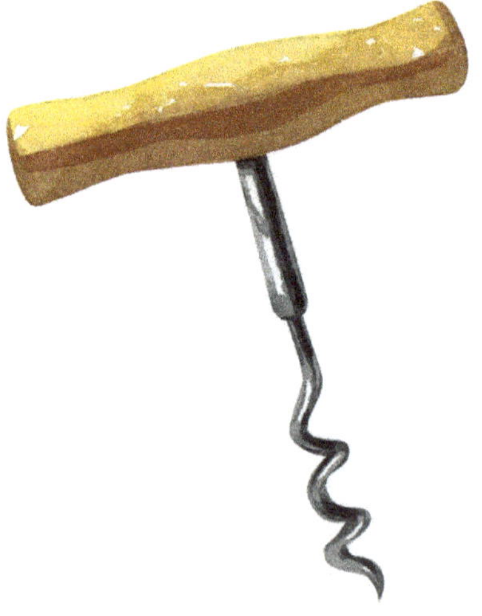

PINOT GRIGIO

Usually, you brush me off and pour me in summer,
but tonight is different.
Tonight is dark, brutal winter.

I rest in your delicate hands, and you review me, remember.
I'm shoved into the cold. But not for long—you can't wait,
so we settle for ice cubes in a mug,
sit outside with your slippers and that rug,
the warmth escaping from the gaps in your robe.

We sit outside, despite the chill. After your ramblings to yourself,
I realize,
why you chose me.

Whether you're trying to remember or trying to forget,
I'll be here,
and even though you may later regret
all these things that have been said,
for now,
I am here,
and I can help those twinkling holiday lights
seem just a bit brighter.

ROSÉ

Oh, stop,
    You make me all rouged
    Bemused
You schmooze, but I love it.

Your silky hair shines under the lamplight, and she just might try
    to give you a wink you'd kill for.

And all the while, a shadow casts across me. Sometimes I forget
    I'm blended—
    Dark with light. Cursed with being fun yet
Deserted. After you go off with your lover, I'll be half emptied,
Nearing the edge of this perfectly marbled counter.

Below, echoes of frenzied feet, meet and greeters, crumbs of the
    evening.

Now I crave for what may be, while I wait to be cleaned,
made anew after this waltz of shame.

SAUVIGNON BLANC

Deep breath—it's just your first time meeting the family.
You're pretending to like me because it's what they offered,
And you won't know this now, but you'll later grow to adore—
    then hate—me.

We squeeze tight onto the couch and converse,
But your hand is a little too tight around my neck. In another
    context
I wouldn't mind—in fact, press a bit harder—
But we're trying to make an impression, here. So don't distract
    me.

Have another sip and offer a friendly tip or anecdote
As an antidote to this painfully amusing process of
"Getting to know."

CHARDONNAY

You and me and him
we're porch sitters
all on a whim
A "hello" across the street
with fireflies sprinkling in navy light

A gesture,
a welcome. A wicker chair, then autumn.
We trade memories like baseball cards.
Exchange pleasantries
and pastries,
and, oh, how I wish to live in your world.

Quiet and natural, screenless
and seamless,
tipsy off of amusement and questions.

Let's porch sit and chat like we always
meant to.

RIESLING

I laugh
because I know how strong
sweetness can be—
    addicting, warm, puzzling, easy
only to throw a punch at the end,
like a love affair.

SPIRITS

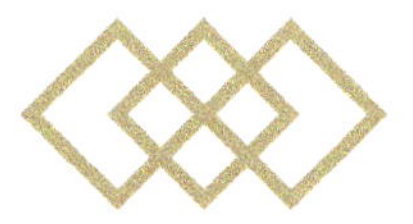

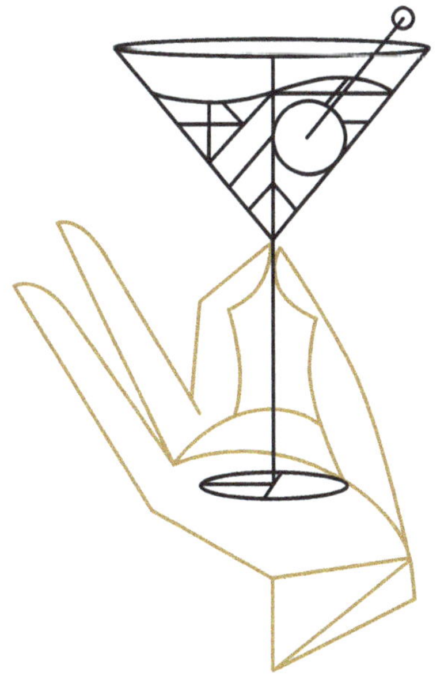

ELDERFLOWER LIQUEUR

Your seat awaits
>At the playwrights' table

Fantasy or not, you'll be whisked away in broad
>Daylight

Only to be enchanted by sirens who pretend you're the Next Big
>Thing.

Even still,
>You'll believe it because

Who can resist the perfect balance of "earthy and lovely"?

GIN

Like you,
I'm far better enjoyed in the company of my fellow mixers.

Alone, I am too strong for most. Repulsive, even.

But blend me with the right kind of saccharine solution and I'll
butter you up right before I blow you away
with the   world's worst
hangover.

And then, who do we blame?
Me, the sugar, or your heartbreak?

VODKA TONIC

One, two, three—and four.
In one cup, out into another.
    Sometimes cradled in a small space
        and licking lots of little cups.
Spilled onto the floor.
That feeling—
    hit, release
    held, fallen
—is that what it's like to be drunk?

APEROL

You are not quite sure, are you?
    It's been a while and,
    even then,
some days you wonder if or when someone finally tells you that
today is still not your day. And that's exactly why you celebrate—
What better way to cut through the boredom of this sun-kissed
    day?

Why waste a beautiful spring night, drowning in your sorrow,
    when you could
    swallow me instead—
Life's scmcn.

What could be sweeter than fucked-up oblivion?

LIMONCELLO

It's been a deliriously delightful, dragged night—or is it
  afternoon?—or morning and it's
either too late or too early to tell but, well, my dear, listen here.
Let's settle and end on a high note, a *C* this time because I
can feel it in my bones.
The zing of my effortless being is a ring on your finger. I devote
  this time to you, this moment that can only get better after
  this—
the bliss
—then soft,
softly, to
sleep.

ESPRESSO MARTINI

Somehow even the most delicate combinations can be
Overdone. Please, ease up your grip and soften your shoulders.
You're alert, but your anxiety stinks up the room,
And we're in the middle of listening to a lovely conversation
     about—
Oh, the waiter is back. And you all banter and flirt
As if he's never seen this before—
A group on the verge of adulthood,
Charmed and flushed with caffeine.
My froth has diluted by the time you finish your story, and now
     we're down to it—
The cutting through the cream and ending with "should we?"

You've taken an institution and made it a mockery.

COSMOPOLITAN

In the heat of it all, your sweat matches the tears slipping down
    my *v*-shaped glass.
Are we crying? Laughing? Writhing with drunk confusion about
what this is?

How I long for a fresh squeeze of lemon
to knife through the poison you call perfume.
Mediocracy is in the periphery—we circle each other, dancing
    martinis, an accidental spill—
Oops, was it *really* my fault?

Sugar or salt? Oh, we forgot the bill. Let's laugh on our way back
    and let the humidity
speak wisdom about how this type of warmth is more
dangerous than the blanket you wear in winter.

Let's fumble for water goblets and swallow the remnants of
    childhood memories, the ones that
burn a little after
you drink them in.

RYE

After all, she was timeless, wasn't
she?
  Etched in diamonds
ever-reflecting the
best and worst parts of you.

  And you loved it,
the way she would
    simmer
    down
    under your touch.
under the stars…

The way she could quiet fireworks with her stare—
"There,"
    in the wind, you
    hear her voice,
thirst in Western dust,
but you decided to move
    on, somewhere, because opportunity sounds more expensive
    than the wide expanse of a soon-to-be-past,
One where her laughter still shadows you like moonshine.

You'll never know if all this time,
     maybe she was laughing at you, and all
     your cowboy façade—because you were never able to handle
     the way
     she could howl
at the night.

SCOTCH ON THE ROCKS

Another rough day.
Here, conduct the fire's flames.
My cold touch to your frustrated, heated hands.
A breath, a breeze. Life back into the body.
A sigh. Pour again, it's okay. Just a splash.
A wave
A downfall.
It's okay. Breathe—
    fire, or ice?

BOURBON

Authority in a glass,
    alas,
I am but a mirror.
Sure, we smile together, but I
can see through your steely eyes
    —*why*—
is a question you ask but never answer, unless someone else is
    asking it because it feels so much better
to
    hint
you know more.

Textbook full of lies, and you
sigh,
claiming to be too tired and yet, here we are, again,
    your mind racing with the same old shit your grandparents
    wondered,
as if you're anything unique.

RUM & COKE

Water isn't the same without a little spice
    especially you, dear, you light up the room
with or without the fine dining and candles.
It takes a special kind of smile to fake that.

Sweet tooth, no?
And did it hurt
    when your tooth was pulled
A flinching reminder that
maybe
it wasn't all so much but
    not enough?

FIREBALL

Hit the bottom, swirl up again.
    Sink deep into liquefied fall.
    We dance around each other—
    Me, the bitter want
    My partner, the hot apple sugar—
Lapping our surrounding walls, sweating with condensation—

I had never wanted to make love
    with such a sweet sensation.

TEQUILA

I roll awake to realize I'm being woken again
Thrown again
Splashed against laughing mouths.
When will my night be over?

ABSINTHE

Neither of us knew what we were in for, but here we are—absent
    and drowning in each other.
Before the paranoia sets in,
Let's take this strange magic and make, create,
mate,
fake that we're not like everyone else. We're not normal, 9-5ers
    with purposeless paychecks.
We don't *succumb* that that kind of world.

We're better than that—we are aware, electrified and terrified
    and
    "What would it bc like to go fight?"
Or maybe we just lounge and stare, soaked in this toxic air, and
    become
    mesmerized by a fire's flames.

BEER

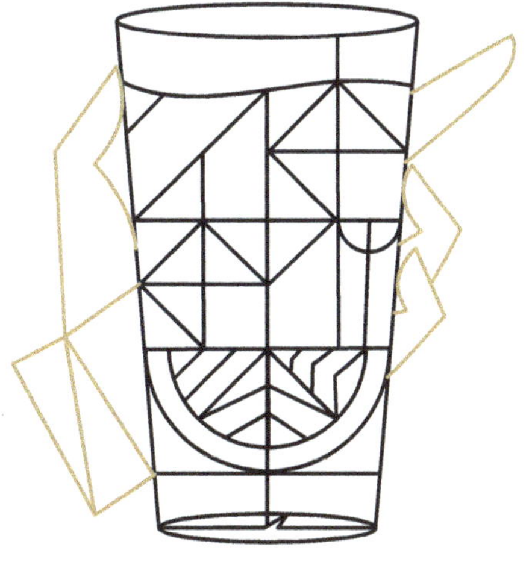

GUINNESS

I,
   am,
    perfection.
Old, bold. I'm not easy,
not like my friends—
they'll serve you all right.
Fast, quick. Where's the fun in that?
No, you must wait.

Patience, please,
as my ruby-black magic
   disperses, spreads, rises to the
occasion.
A soft bubble of foam—the kind that reminds
you
of milk mustaches
   whipped cream-topped hot chocolate
    warm nights.

And now look at you—
how proudly you hold, bold, entitled.
Lick your lips again, clean off the milky white.
How tightly you squeeze,
   how light you feel.
   Like you could be a kid again.

Lick those lips. Waiting is harder the second time 'round.

To youth!
To naivety!
To impatience and curiosity!

The longer you wait, the more you become
    what you cheer to.

IPA

Fake liking me to impress your friends
or enjoy every last drop because when the sun hits just right, on
    that kind of night,
something about a cold one—even when you've been the cold
    one
with a shoulder icier than the arctic—

At least there is this—*whatever this is*—
and your mother's
voice in the back of your head and that vision
you had and that memory of gym class,
roaming high school halls,
never wondering at all what this moment might be like—you,
older and not as wise,
    repeating
        these
                nightly
        routines
not because I'm your toxic habit,
but familiarity is.

You always went for what was safer.
Hiding behind your accolades.
Still, a trace of me and your past at the back of your tongue,
a tantalizing gag because maybe the anticipation of something
    awful is just as great
as something sweet, so…you
veto the wine—
    though we both know it tastes
so
    much
        better.

PUMPKIN ALE

I'm thirsting for the type of you that comes out
When the air turns crisp
The you that milks each minute under candlelight

I watch your hands rest on the
Oak bar
Fingertips kissing the cracks
I miss that anticipation—the evening before
The evening, the nerves before the party

Where I'll see you, cinnamon dusted on your lips from tasting
    the cider you made.

We were born,
For the first break, the leaf-crack of fall.
The curious wait for the magical flakes of the season.

Forget all rhyme and reason,
Intrigue traps me now
And you've cast a good one on me.

I'll be here, waiting for you, at the end of the
Masquerade, and drape your blanket over you.

KÖLSCH

The moon's sideways smile
might be the only one they see
among a sea of faraway eyes and
trails of empty laughter.

STELLA ARTOIS

Sneak me out of your parents' mini fridge
    and tell me your secrets.
    I admit this—
You are lost to him.

But there's nothing wrong with a little flirtation—a little longing
and song-sending
and starry skies with him on your mind.

You're wasted, and I'm just a small part of that. Despite the
    honor, it's more fun watching you test the far ends
of this strayed,
dismayed,
horribly conveyed,
romantic dramedy that you've latched onto.

I shouldn't judge you.
I only notice the rare occasions in which you choose me
from of all the expensive liquor in this house.

And I realize that I'm no real threat—instead, I'm a seducing buzz
    and a tickle in your ear. You hold me with such nonchalance
    that even I have become more casual these days.

Watching you in this haze—the adorable ways you send your
    favorite memories or songs to him. In this moment, we belong.

BELGIUM BLONDE ALE

Never a wrong choice but rarely right, you wonder
if maybe there's something better on the other side
    of the bar,
the building, the
street,
the bridge.

And it's there, waiting—
a sunset over a future only you imagined.
Maybe it will always seem nicer that way. An unknown
only you can cultivate
while you hold your love in your hands
    a bubbly intoxication that grows
flatter with each sip.

And it's easier,
maybe, to be the
same as him. In some way,
there's honor there, in the consistency,
the way it flows from one generation to the next.
    And what's wrong with that? In fact,
things may be much worse
    in the wrong hands.

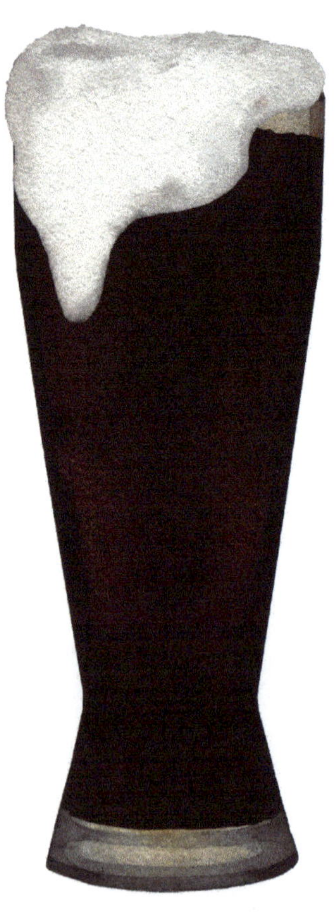

PORTER

I wish,
or thought,
you would see me as equally
creative,
 intelligent,
but I was willing
to impress you.

Now, I know you've etched a small history into my youth,
and today I find myself showing you something else—someone
 unafraid.

Is it the confidence now that turns you on, or the fact that I've
 had other lovers, and you—
  you weren't my first?

SOUR

Why not?
Be finicky.
And see,
maybe,
your particular taste in men isn't just as
     ridiculous
as you make it seem.

Here, take off that clown makeup—it'll smear sooner or later,
from your tears
or his lips.
What would it be like to just sit in your
Never-ending silence for once?

Can you tune into the soft ways the stars still speak to you?
Maybe you can cut the bitter
with your own version of sweet.

Sure—it'll taste like shit at first.
But so did every other drink before this one.
What's a little bite ever do to you?

THE HANGOVER

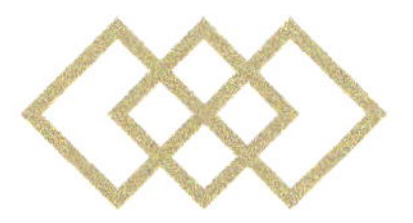

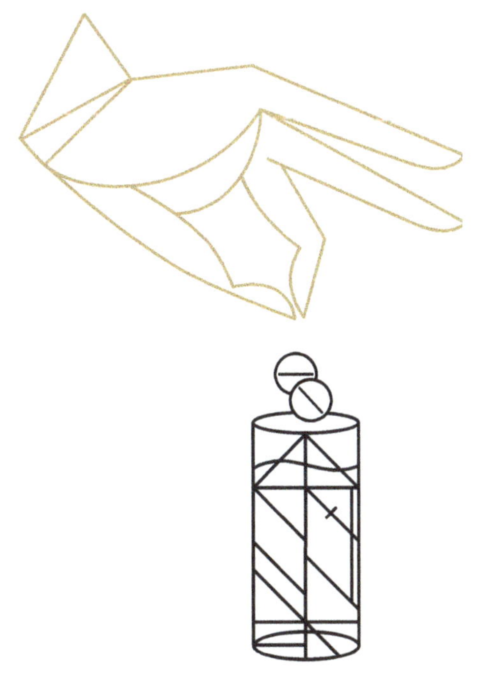

THE NEXT MOURNING

Why do next-day tears—
salty with regret and longing—
taste like sweet wine
you know you'll regret again later?

SUN DRUNK

The haze is my new conquest
How dare I dive into the water's honey reflection
or float along crests like a dragonfly?
I'll take those rays any day
over the way I once lay
    on the bathroom floor—staring at that pond that judges me
    from the toilet.

It's funny how easily the
sunlight brings such peace,
when my world before was fear-mongering and dark,
    a thunderstorm that ached for me to be home
    and a hurricane of thoughts that stripped me to my core.
At least out here, in these waters, I have
    turtles and cranes to call my friends.

Oh, apples—they do fall further away than you'd think.

WHISKEY DREAMS

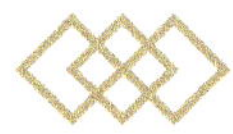

Two shots of whiskey and a
Dreaded red sofa away—
I take three and conduct a scolding array of flames with
My cobblestone worn boots. A grimy piece of
Napkin naps in my corner.
    Or is it nestled?

                                Down the first.

        'Course, words have
        Visual.
"Nestle" settles.
    "Nap" sinks.
Does it matter now?

                            Down the second.

        Not unless it did, or does. But no lad would
        Call a napkin napping.
Two in and a blurry mind—I'm still deciding which is better?

A napkin is a napkin. It doesn't eat
Away
Crumbs of dreams.

Is this napkin brushing crumbs, or displaying my own?

Unless—I, myself, am a cliché.

If I look, my words could change.

I'm too ashamed of my answer to pick up the next.

SIMPLE SYRUP

Speaking of, the buzz,
It's strong—the kind that smacks,
dizzying bees. My knees,
wobbling and falling over for you, tripped up by the words you
    say and the things you try to hold back

It's never the same,
to me
it goes from

sugarcoated to
de leche—
crème de la crème,
    sorbet—

all a different taste of you

The grind of sugar cubes between fingertips,
    viscous honey,
whispers of powdered sugar shaken over me like secrets,
the clap of the spoon against crème brûlée—

    the sound of you, it remains.

You are the bubbles freshly popped, and the squeeze of a
    strawberry
when you press it into my mouth.
All of you, it strums like music in summer twilight.
You are the birds' melodies that haunt and scatter and call for
    me in the wind.

You're the comfort of resting in an old couch, that heavenly, easy
    fall.

Witness the show that comes with showering in champagne. You,
    bubbles in my veins—
shocking my system with intoxicating questions, compliments.
Oh, the unknown of what it all really means—the way it strangely
    makes more sense with more time—like wine, bottles of you
    are lost to me.

You—your clothes fallen like popped corks left on the floor.

You—you unravel me.

SOBER SEX

Here I thought
my trusted truth serum would hide the lie that—no, I'm chill.
    "Seeking thrill."
I didn't realize that butterflies could be part of the fun,
since it never was.

Dopamine for you, a weapon to me.

These days when I drink
I think
about rape—what it is, isn't.

"At least he didn't force you."
It's like I'm special, lucky.
So why do I dream that I'm trapped,
wake up gasping for breath—and not in the good ways, where I
    want your hands
around my neck?

Maybe I didn't have it so bad.
The sleeping pills felt better, because to you, at least, I seemed
    light and free.

And now I drink because my body is ruined
from the stress and strain of not knowing how I really felt.

Now I drink, and I don't know what the nerves mean
What it's like to like—
Or maybe I do, but it's easier to coat them with wine.

At least I won't lie to myself.
For now, it's simpler this way. And if a day comes when butterflies
    become my Chardonnay then maybe,
I'll stray,
just a little, toward what it's like to trust
again.

COLD SHOWERS

Like soap—
    she tried to clean others'
    messes,
only to lose herself in the
process.

HUNGOVER IN BED WITH YOU

Butterfly kisses on a cold morning,
    on cheeks dewy from last night's tears,
      on skin I've picked apart,
        on a surface that hides the erosion
        inside,
on scars left behind.

Your strokes like a feather on a
broken bird, a quiet reminder
that all is not lost.

TOUCH ME WHEN I'M LOW

The drops of dew slip from the curves of such
Soft branches, thudding against the pond below
and splashing repeatedly as if they were
    a bass; the ripples casting, sending waves
Throughout the body. Petal-soft kisses
will find my waxy skin of leaves, and so
I roll my hands to where her short and curved
hills meet. The flowered fingers crawl into
    my winded breath and stretch to where our
hands
Connect. And oh, can I not see, arching,
Hovered before me; a wooing womanly tree,
a chest that rises slowly; an overhanging
               canopy? A smooth, curved hole beneath
my shaking hands, the hardwood floor—the
black and cherry, white and ash, red oak, dripped
sap.

To think that I have found just one in all
the brush; and yet I do not ponder, "Could I
have climbed some more?"

GREASY FOOD

Salt never tasted so sweet.
We lay here, in victorious defeat,
Watching the TV.
After a few hours of delirium and sleep
My brain and body ask,
More dopamine, please.

The high from the night before
Breathes under my fingertips, stretched
Across your chest,
In your bark-hued hair
In tired eyes.
It's in the crumbled bag of takeout and the
Sun finally setting again.

But even this moment, I know, will pass. And
I'll hang onto the way you looked at me
Instead of the shots
To get me through the rest of the day, the
Week, the month before you decide to leave.

And now I buy greasy food when I'm missing
You.

THE WALK HOME FROM THE BAR

After a time,
The shade of afternoon sun starts to shift
    in a way that
hushes
down
rather than screams out, "Goodbye"

We're weaving together now, that honey light enhancing my
    gentle glow of the grape.
    Jazz doesn't sound the same now that
I've rid it of your name. In fact,
It sounds better, and I can savor the melodies without your
    memories
guilt tripping me in that classic way—to everyone else

    You sir, are saintly. God-sent. Unquestionably right and
    life-saving.

I had no grounds to question, or even mention
        the slight possibility   you couldn't fix me.

It's more fun to appear a martyr than agree to change your ways.
But you will continue to be the hero for your collective fan club,
    in love
    with your charisma, the kind you hide from us because you
    "don't like attention."
If only they knew—how monstrous those hands could be outside
    the mask of your controlled setting.
If only they heard how loud you could get when your strings were
    pulled just right,
    triggered to become a dark soul no one's seen.

God forbid I question you, or react to your
    underreactions.
You claim to know and yet you flounder and waiver—
    stuck on whoever made you look your best. Remorse and
    regret
are not pretty, and you never made your pride in me louder than
    your pride in yourself.

Oh, how you can conduct a band with the easiest flick of your
    fucking hand.
Everyone is glad to follow along, to you and the books you gave
    them.
    I stand aside, away, finally ignited
By my own music—sounds only I can create—I stand, the notes
    unable to infiltrate and manipulate
like sirens.
I stand, uninterested in the music you continue to play.

And you know, don't you? How it kills us both, a little inside,
All "feelings" aside.

I won't waver, even if you do, or pretend to.
And now, I've got instrumental tools at my disposal—a choir of
    friends who have nothing
to lose in protecting me—
    Something you never could do.

Though my words have been twisted—
the truth,
    this   graphite—
remains honest.
I questioned it always, the authenticity in these words—words!
If only my story rang true. But now I know that not all audiences
    are the same,

    and that justice, though rarely loud,
breathes down my fingers as I write.

SECRETS FROM THE SPEAKEASY

Youth is in the ways your gaze lights and turns away—casting
  looks to meaningless edges of my corner.
To watch without watching.
To smile without noticing.
Is it really a rarity to notice?

To take note and look, longingly, with a kind of hope that nudges
  you along with the sunshine—
Its complement, its excuse to use every energy you have toward
  something more than what is.

A coupe of "what could be," would be—if only the one you
  wanted would drink you in like June at midnight.
Glistened by lightning bugs who tend to you when you're
  overcome with bliss.
The fountain waters show who you are—right now, without fail
  or question.

It might be that the way you look at that water is what makes it
  truly
  remarkable.

You—witnessing the glow of you, without effort, just curiosity.
We sway with delirium, humming, drinking and dazzled and
      dazed in the way we create a
      sort of replication of
Nature. If it rains, we embrace the softness that comes after a
      storm. Dewy, not wilted.
Wishing well that our pennies that fell earlier spoke some truth.

We are aimless with intention. This—an invention, of what is and
      yet to be. We see a world that asks us to paint with colors
      given, with flirtations arisen, that kind of color
      that is bioluminescent.

I try, with small might, to draw in your eye. The magnet is stronger
      with passerby who may not be aware of your spell.
Pretending to ignore the way you speed by without wonder—I
      wonder, what is truly crossing one's mind when we find such
      gentle but large ways to hide.

We exchange softness in silence, the kind that asks for more.

ACKNOWLEDGEMENTS

Writing is not always a pleasant hobby, despite how much I love it. It can eat at you, make you question your worth, but also empower you and change your life. These moments are often projected onto my support system, the people of which I will recognize in detail below in no particular order.

This collection began when I took a poetry class in college with Spring Ulmer. Her teaching was exactly the opposite of what I feared a poetry class would be—ultra highbrow and all-knowing, classist, pretentious, judgmental. I submitted a much shorter version of this collection as a final project. Her support and feedback created the initial spark that helped me feel like I could be a true poet. Years later, I resurrected my old writings and decided to expand on them, and they've become this much larger project. I want to thank her and all of my teachers and professors for their wisdom, softness, and encouragement. From grade school to college, I was lucky enough to have incredible support from so many of my teachers, whether they were in the English department or not.

I'd like to specifically thank Jeanine O'Brien Waldron, my high school English teacher, who encouraged me to submit my work to the Scholastic Art and Writing Awards when I was just a teenager. It was the first time I would enter my work into a contest. She helped me through the documentation, the process, and nudged me to submit despite being a quiet, shy writer in her class. She saw something in me and pushed me to see where my talent would go. Little did we know my work would be nationally recognized and celebrated at Carnegie Hall among the rest of the artists. It was the first time I realized that my writing meant something more, something outside of myself.

I wouldn't have been so inspired and motivated to keep up with writing if it weren't for some key colleagues (and friends) of mine. These are the people who have seen my work over the many years and/or have provided me with resources and networking advice. They spent their precious time reviewing my work—from random ramblings to novels to *Dear Daughter* to this project and more. They have lifted me up when I felt low or doubted my skills, and their passion and enthusiasm rejuvenated me during depression droughts. These folks include Lara Herreid, Charlie O. Delune, K. Goss, Lauren McClusick, Violet James McMaster, and Joe Sweeney.

Finally, thank you to my dear, close friends for their emotional support and cheerleading. They've seen me when I had no spirit left. They've seen me when we've shared spirits together. They've witnessed my happiness and peace, my fears and my heartbreak and pain. Not only did they read and support drafts of *Dear Daughter* and *Poisons,* they've read my diary entries, my text messages, and my body language. They are like family, and I feel every writer needs a home base to fall back on. They've accepted all of me, flaws and all, and that inspired me to pursue my work with confidence. Thank you, so much, to my friends (family), in no special order: Alli Kanarish, Kinjal Shah, Samantha Helias, and Nick and Morgan Tate.

ABOUT THE AUTHOR

A linguistics scholar and mental health advocate, Samantha Mineroff has been writing creatively since she first held a pencil. Her novella was nationally recognized by Scholastic during the 2013 Scholastic Art and Writing Awards. She became a passionate academic, winning the 2018 Best Seminar Paper Award for her paper "The Rhetoric of Major Depressive Disorder: Performativity and Intra-activity of Emotions in Major Depression." She was a recipient of the Viola Marple Scholarship and the *Daedalus* Poetry Award, and she coauthored the paper, "Interpersonal touch and the achievement of shared understanding in English conversation," which was presented at the Language and Social Interaction Working Group conference at Teachers College, Columbia.

After graduating from West Chester University with an English degree and dual minors in creative writing and linguistics, her professional writing grew and was featured on numerous mental health platforms. In 2019, she presented her research on negative accommodation theory at the University of Liverpool during the Poetics and Linguistics Association conference. At just twenty-three years old, she was of the youngest to present.

When she isn't writing or researching, you'll find her listening to live music, singing and strumming a guitar, strolling through parks, and traveling the globe.

Photo taken by Bryan MacNeill of Son Of Neill Aesthetics
Instagram: @sonofneill_aesthetics